Zora Neale Hurston

D1522855

Painting of Zora by Diego Caillet

Zora Neale Hurston

Wrapped in Rainbows

Sandra Wallus Sammons

Pineapple Press, Inc.
Sarasota, Florida

Dedicated to my dear friend and fellow librarian, Barbara Shew. Our lives have been made richer by the life and writings of Zora Neale Hurston.

Inquiries should be addressed to:
Pineapple Press, Inc.
P.O. Box 3889
Sarasota, Florida 34230

www.pineapplepress.com

Library of Congress Cataloging-in-Publication Data

Sammons, Sandra Wallus.
    Zora Neale Hurston : wrapped in rainbows / by Sandra Wallus Sammons.
    pages   cm.
    ISBN 978-1-56164-683-8 (hardcover : alk. paper)
    ISBN 978-1-56164-682-1 (pbk. : alk. paper)
    1. Hurston, Zora Neale—Juvenile literature. 2. Novelists, American—20th century—Biography—Juvenile literature. 3. Folklorists—United States—Biography—Juvenile literature. 4. African American novelists—Biography—Juvenile literature. 5. African American women—Biography—Juvenile literature. I. Title.

PS3515.U789Z84 2014
813'.52—dc23
[B]
                                                              2013039101

First Edition
10 9 8 7 6 5 4 3 2 1

Design by Shé Hicks
Cover painting: oil portrait of Zora commissioned by *The Orlando Sentinel* and
    painted by artist Diego Caillet
Printed in the United States

"Well, that is the way things stand up to now. I can look back and see sharp shadows, highlights, and smudgy in-betweens. I have been in Sorrow's kitchen and licked out all the pots. Then I have stood on the peaky mountain wrapped in rainbows, with a harp and a sword in my hands."

—*Dust Tracks on a Road*

Contents

Foreword

Zora Neale Hurston once said, "Sometimes, I feel discriminated against, but it does not make me angry. It merely astonishes me. How *can* any deny themselves the pleasure of my company?"

These were strange words from an African-American woman living in America in the early 1900s, when many men and women of her race were angry about the way they were treated. But Zora Neale Hurston was different. She was proud and happy to be alive and to be African-American! She wrote four novels, two books of folklore, her autobiography, short stories, plays, and articles, many of them celebrating life and the African-American culture.

When she died in 1960, her books were out of print and hard to find. Today they can be found in many schools and libraries, and her life has been honored in many ways. In 1990 Zora was included in the Florida Artists Hall of

Fame, and an annual celebration of her life was begun in the Florida cities of Eatonville and Fort Pierce.

Zora Neale Hurston, author from the small town of Eatonville, Florida, has been called "one of the greatest writers of the twentieth century" and has inspired writers of all races around the world.

Chapter 1

A Very Special Town

Zora was born on January 7, 1891, the fifth in a family of eight children. At the time of her birth, many changes were happening in the lives of African-Americans.

Zora's grandparents had been slaves. Freed by the Emancipation Proclamation of 1863, that generation had not been allowed to go to school. Zora's parents, John and Lucy Hurston, did learn to read and write, but they were working on a cotton plantation in Notasulga, Alabama, when she was born.

John Hurston traveled south, hoping to find a better place to raise his children. In most places, he found black and white families living together within a city but separated in different areas. Then John heard about

Eatonville, an entire town in Florida that had been founded as an all–African-American community. He decided to see it for himself. He liked what he saw, and it would be their home.

Nearby Maitland, a white community in central Florida, had been built by black laborers. The African-Americans, however, lived in a town that was built about a mile away. It was called Eatonville to honor the white businessman, Josiah Eaton, who helped them obtain the land.

Maitland became an official city in 1885, and Eatonville was formed just two years later, in 1887. Both Maitland and Eatonville elected a mayor and a marshal. The big difference was that in Eatonville, all of the elected officials were African-American men. Eatonville became the first incorporated, self-governing African-American town in America.

Zora's family moved to Eatonville when she was three years old. In the new town, she had African-American friends and neighbors, and the color of her skin was the same as theirs. She knew for sure that she could do anything at all with her life. She did not have to conform to what others wanted her to do. She said later in her autobiography, "I am so put together that I do not have much of a herd instinct. Or if I must be connected

City seal of Eatonville, Florida, 1999 (State Archives of Florida, Florida Memory, http://floridamemory.com/items/show/124216, photographed by Tina Bucuvalas)

with the flock, let *me* be the shepherd my ownself. That is just the way I am made."

Zora's family had a respected place in town. John Hurston was a fine carpenter who had saved enough money to buy five acres of land right in the heart of Eatonville. He built a large, eight-room house close to Macedonia Baptist Church, where he preached, and the

Hungerford School, which his children attended. He was elected mayor of Eatonville three times.

The family's large garden provided good food. Fruit trees in their yard supplied them with grapefruit, oranges, tangerines, and guava. Fish filled the clear, clean lakes in town. If the children were hungry, they would collect eggs from the chickens roaming the yard and hard-boil them. Whatever they didn't eat, they'd have fun throwing at each other!

Their home was along a dirt road that took travelers into Maitland or Orlando. Rich white people driving by in their fancy cars would notice the lovely gardens, with sweet-smelling Cape Jasmine bushes lining the walkway to the house and the two large chinaberry trees in the yard.

Zora loved her large family, but she and her father were never close. He would ask Zora why she couldn't be more like her sister Sarah, who was quiet and respectful. Zora was polite, but she was always her own individual, outgoing self. Instead of taking her father's advice, Zora listened to her mother and did her best to live life to the fullest.

Zora's father, John Hurston
(State Archives of Florida, Florida
Memory, http://floridamemory.com/items/
show/35828)

Chapter 2

Growing Up in Eatonville

Zora and her mother, Lucy Ann Potts Hurston, were very close. Zora was sure that she was her favorite child. Lucy knew that her youngest daughter was very smart and did what she could to make the most of the young girl's talents.

Education was very important to Lucy Hurston. Her children could read and write even before they attended school. She would gather all of them into her bedroom and help them with their lessons. If the homework went beyond her knowledge, the older children helped the younger ones.

Once Zora learned how to read, she didn't want to stop. Suddenly, she found new worlds opening up. She

Principal's house at the Robert Hungerford Normal and Industrial School, Eatonville, Florida (State Archives of Florida, Florida Memory, http://floridamemory.com/items/show/2728)

read every book she could, from cover to cover. When she was naughty, she was sent to her mother's room as punishment. She loved being sent there, though, because then she could spend hours reading her mother's Bible. She read with great delight about heroes like David and Moses and Herod the Great.

Lucy Hurston would not "squinch" her daughter's spirit. Although small in size, she stood up to her husband when he said, "It [does] not do for Negroes to have too much spirit." Lucy wanted her children to grow up knowing they were special. She told them to "jump at de sun," meaning that she wanted them to be the best they could be. Zora realized, "We might not land on the sun, but at least we would get off the ground."

Young Zora was full of curiosity about her world. She sat in one of the two big chinaberry trees in her front yard and dreamed about what lay at the end of the dirt road going past her house. Her mother explained this longing to see the rest of the world by saying that surely someone had sprinkled "travel dust" on the doorstep when Zora was born.

Zora also loved to meet new people. She sat on the gatepost in front of her house, waiting for a fancy car to pass by. She waved and asked if the people would like her to ride with them for a bit. When they invited her to climb in, Zora sang and told stories for about half a mile. She then got out of the car and walked home, hoping her parents had not missed her. She was sure to get a scolding—or worse—if they found out that she had been riding with strangers again!

Zora asked many questions and loved to make up stories. She had seen a bird, she said, with a very long tail sitting high up in the tall pine tree in their yard. The tail, "all blue and pink and red and green," was so long that it reached all the way to the ground. When Zora told her mother about this wonderful bird, her mother smiled and listened patiently.

During the day, Zora walked barefoot through the nearby woods, where she sang and talked to the trees and animals. When the moon came out at night, Zora was convinced that the moon followed her because she was so special. A lot of her time was spent alone because she didn't like playing girls' games and her parents didn't want her to play with rough boys. She created her own little playmates from odds and ends she found around the house.

She spent hours with Miss Corn Shuck, which was really the covering of an ear of corn. Mr. Sweet Smell was Miss Corn Shuck's friend. He was a bar of sweet-smelling soap that she found in her mother's bureau drawer and that was reserved for guests. She made up one story after another about these two "people" and their adventures.

If she wanted to hear stories, Joe Clarke's general store was the place for that. Before the days of radio or television, neighbors would gather at the store in the center of town for a good time. Men would sit for hours, telling stories about what used to be or tales they made up. Each man would try to tell the wildest, most exaggerated story ever. For example, someone describing a very strong wind might say, "It blowed a crooked road straight." Now that would be some strong wind!

Zora spent as much time as she could listening to the men using their imagination. Sometimes one would play a guitar or harmonica and sing some lively songs, and she loved tapping her feet to the music. Joe Clarke's store was an exciting place. She only left because she knew her parents wanted her back home.

Zora loved her little community, but somehow she always felt she was different from the other children her age. She said later, "True, I played, fought and studied with other children, but always I stood apart within." She would always be her own person. She was determined to "jump at de sun."

By fifth grade, Zora was very good at reading. When two white women visited the all-black Hungerford School, Zora's class was asked to read aloud for them. When Zora's turn came, she read a story from Greek mythology with such feeling that the visitors were very impressed. She was asked to read for them again at their hotel in Maitland.

Her mother made sure Zora was well-scrubbed and wearing shoes for the visit. The women were so delighted with this charming African-American girl who could read so well that they gave her a hundred shiny new pennies to take home. She received another present in the mail. The women had sent a large box filled with books and clothes. Now Zora could read her *own* books! She particularly enjoyed *Gulliver's Travels* and the Greek, Roman, and Norse myths.

The exciting books made her want, even more, to see the world. Although she loved her home and family, she later said, "My soul was with the gods and my body in the village." Her busy, happy childhood would remain in her memory for the rest of her life. It would also become a part of the stories she would write, one after another, through the years.

Chapter 3

"A Little Colored Girl"

Zora's happy life changed when her mother died. Later she would describe her feelings: "Mama died at sundown and changed a world." At age 13, Zora had lost the one person in the world who knew her best.

John Hurston was unable to care for the children still at home, so Zora was sent to the school in Jacksonville, Florida, where her older brother and sister, Bob and Sarah, were studying. Just two weeks after her mother died, Zora packed her belongings into an old suitcase. She boarded the train alone, heading north from Maitland.

Gone were the protection and the love she had felt in her hometown. "Jacksonville made me know that I was a little colored girl," she wrote later. She had been sent

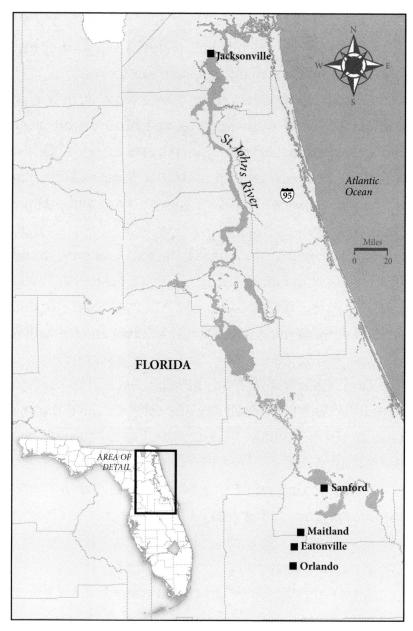

Map of Northeast Florida (Jennifer Borresen)

to live in a large, segregated city. She no longer had all African-American friends and relatives supporting her. Life in Eatonville had not prepared her for this.

At least she was in a place where there were books, and classes went well. Reading and history were easy for her, but she called math "an unnecessary evil." When a spelling bee was held for all of the African-American schools in Jacksonville, Zora won an atlas and a Bible for first prize.

But her stay at the Florida Baptist Academy would be short. Within months of her mother's death, her father had remarried. Twenty-year-old Mattie Moge Hurston wanted nothing to do with John's children, and her father stopped paying Zora's room and board at school.

Zora chose to finish off the school year, but she had to pay her own way. Each day after classes she did some cleaning in the kitchen, and each Saturday she scrubbed the school stairs.

At the beginning of summer vacation, she was told to wait until her father picked her up to take her home. He never came. She was finally given $1.50 so she could board a boat going south, taking her home.

Alone on the huge riverboat called the *City of Jacksonville,* she still made the most of the experience. As she traveled south on the St. Johns River, at least she was seeing something of the world. She didn't go hungry either. The waiter on board was friendly and sent her to the back of the steamboat with plates of chicken, pie, and cake.

The boat docked in Sanford, and she took the train to Maitland. She made her way to Eatonville, and there she walked through a familiar doorway. But this was no longer "home." She was sent away to live for five long years in the homes of friends or relatives. Most of the people she lived with didn't see much value in continuing her education. She said later about this time: "I was doing none of the things I wanted to do."

She realized now that she was totally responsible for making something of her life. She *would* get her education. She *would* find books to read. She *would*, somehow, see the rest of the world. She said, "I had a way of life inside me and I wanted it with a want that was twisting me." She would not give up wanting to "jump at de sun."

Finally, a friend told her about an interesting job. An actress with an operetta company was looking for a "lady's maid," someone to help get her costumes ready for each performance. The friend provided a lovely blue dress with a white collar for the interview. The actress liked Zora immediately and hired her. The job was perfect.

Zora earned $10 a week and traveled from city to city. The company performed in musical plays written by the popular English writers and composers W.S. Gilbert and Arthur Sullivan. Fascinated, Zora watched the audiences enjoy the lively music and stories. Zora might not be in school, but she was learning lessons in real life about music and writing and art.

The actress, whom we know only as Miss M, decided to get married and leave the operetta company while they were in Baltimore, Maryland. Giving Zora a small amount of money when they parted, Miss M encouraged Zora to go back to school. She realized this young girl was very intelligent.

Again Zora would have to figure out the next step in her life.

Chapter 4

Finally, an Education

In the early 1900s, America was changing constantly. New roads and train tracks crossed the nation, leading to new states that were still being added to the Union. Unfortunately, for African-Americans things did not change so quickly. Zora had seen segregation in Jacksonville, and she had found that African-Americans were not always welcome, particularly in Southern states. If she wanted a high school education, she would have to look for a school for African-Americans.

Zora was 26 years old. She had learned to take care of herself. When she found out that public schools in Maryland were free to students under the age of 20, Zora registered, saying she was 16. She had always looked younger than her real age. Evidently her plan worked, because she was asked to take an entrance examination to see if she was capable of doing high school work.

Passing the entrance exam was easy, and she was accepted into the junior class. A room and job were found for her at the home of one of the trustees of the school. Zora loved living there. The trustee had a large library, and Zora was given permission to read the books. She read everything she could and even memorized parts of the books because she was afraid she wouldn't ever see them again. She said later, "I acted as if the books would run away."

She particularly loved her English literature classes. Zora already had learned the power of music and theater. In high school, her teachers inspired her by reading stories and poetry, and she came to love words. Satisfied to finally be back in school, Zora said later, "Every new thing I learned in school made me happy."

She studied hard, but she also needed a sense of humor. Her classmates kidded her about what she would wear the next day. She owned only one dress, one change of underclothes, and one pair of tan shoes, so Zora just laughed along with her friends. Her classmates were kind, though. When the school had a special program, the girls gladly loaned her one of their dresses.

Zora did so well in English and history classes that she was sometimes asked to teach the class when the teacher was away. She enjoyed science too, but she still could not make sense of math. She graduated with her high school degree in June 1918. She had planned to apply to Morgan State College, also in Baltimore. She now had this tremendous interest in words and music and theater. She wanted to become a writer!

When she told her friend Mae Miller about her plans, Mae had another idea. Perhaps Zora should apply to the school she was attending in Washington, D.C., Howard University. The nation's capital at that time might also be a more comfortable place for Zora to live. Large groups of African-Americans were moving from Southern states to Northern states, looking for better jobs. This movement of thousands of people from the South to the North was called the Great Migration.

Mae's parents paid Zora's way to Washington, D.C., and she stayed with them for a while. After taking some classes to prepare her for college, Zora proudly entered Howard University in the fall of 1919.

She chose morning classes so she could work from 3:30 P.M. until 8:30 P.M as a waitress and manicurist to pay for her tuition, books, and living expenses. Then it was time to do homework. She greatly respected her teachers and loved learning at this excellent school. Later she said, "I felt the ladder under my feet."

Zora wrote some stories, and her professors and her classmates noticed her talent. She received an invitation to become a member of Howard's writing club. One of her stories, "John Redding Goes to Sea," was printed in the May 1921 issue of *The Stylus,* the club's magazine. Like Zora in real life, John Redding wanted to leave his hometown to see the world, but he also didn't want to leave his family.

She loved writing, but she also had a major distraction—handsome Herbert Sheen.

Herbert was a medical student at Howard, and Herbert and Zora fell deeply in love. They later married, but the marriage didn't last long. Zora had too much she wanted to accomplish in life to settle down. There would be other love affairs too, but her passion for learning and writing were always urging her on.

For five years she worked and took classes part-time, but Zora completed only one and a half years of college credits and was out of money again. How would she complete her education and make the most of her writing ability?

Fortunately, there was help available. Groups were being formed to help African-Americans get an education and jobs and make the most of their lives. The National Urban League was encouraging black artists by publishing a magazine called *Opportunity: A Journal of Negro Life.* Dr. Charles S. Johnson was the editor, and he was publishing work by African-American writers that was not seen in other magazines.

Zora sent one of her stories, "Drenched in Light," to Dr. Johnson. When you read this story, you will recognize little Isie Watts, the main character. She is a "little brown figure perched upon the gatepost" in a town between Orlando and Sanford in Florida. Does she sound familiar? Little Isie, like young Zora, would ask for rides from strangers going by her house. Zora was writing from her memory, making a story from events that actually happened.

Johnson recognized Zora's talent. He published her story in the December 1924 issue of *Opportunity.* A new door had opened for the young woman from Eatonville, Florida. Dr. Johnson also mentioned that Zora should think about moving to New York City.

Chapter 5

A Fresh Start in Harlem

With a few clothes and some half-written stories, Zora headed north. This move particularly took a lot of courage. On a cold day in January 1925 she arrived in the big city of New York. She was a single black woman, 34 years old, with no job, no place to live, and only $1.50 in her pocket. Only her confidence and her dreams were leading her on!

At the offices of the National Urban League on East 23rd Street, she was warmly welcomed by Dr. Johnson. *Opportunity*'s offices were in Manhattan, one of the five boroughs that make up New York City. Just north of 23rd Street is a section of Manhattan called Harlem. During the Great Migration, Harlem became the largest urban black community in America.

Harlem was a wonderful place for black artists. Talented painters, poets, musicians, and writers were all together in one small part of New York City. Black cooks started new restaurants in Harlem, featuring black-eyed peas and Southern fried chicken on their menus. There was new, toe-tapping music. Duke Ellington and Louis Armstrong were playing jazz and the blues in Harlem's many clubs, like the Cotton Club. Historians would later call this period the Harlem Renaissance.

So it was in Harlem where Zora rented an apartment. Feeling comfortable again and having many friends, Zora soon became one of the most popular personalities in town. People began repeating "Zora stories" all over Harlem. She rarely drank alcohol, but one of her friends said, "When Zora was there, she *was* the party!" She loved wearing hats. She wore slacks, something most ladies did not wear at that time. She once said, "I am just running wild in every direction, trying to see everything at once."

Her apartment was usually filled with people talking, singing, and laughing, with Zora at the center of it all. But if she had a story on her mind, the party went on without her. She would go into the bedroom, close the door, and work.

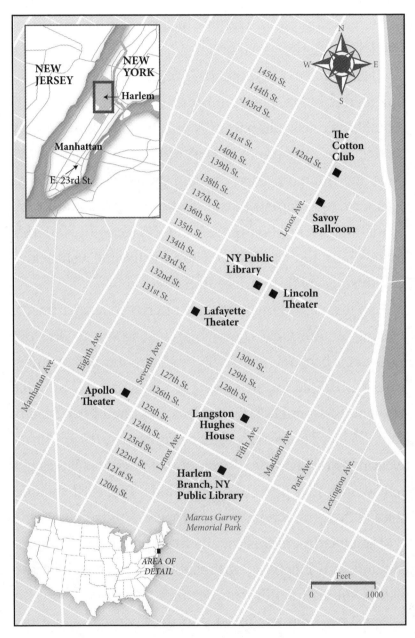

Map of Harlem in New York City (Jennifer Borresen)

She had success with her writing in New York. When the editors of *Opportunity* magazine decided to have their first literary contest, Dr. Johnson encouraged Zora to enter some of her work. Out of hundreds of entries by other writers, both her short story "Spunk" and her play *Color Struck* won second prize in their categories.

The awards ceremony for the contest was on May 1, 1925, and Zora totally enjoyed the evening. Never a shy person, she walked in and announced herself with a big, wide smile, saying, "Color Struuuck" in a loud voice, and threw a brightly colored scarf around her neck. People noticed when Zora entered a room!

At the dinner, Zora was hailed as one of the most promising new talents among African-American writers. There were about 300 people at the festivities, and some of those people would be very helpful to Zora in her career.

Fannie Hurst was there. Already a well-known writer, Ms. Hurst mentioned that she was looking for a secretary. She asked Zora to work for her, but they soon found Zora to be a terrible secretary. She couldn't type. She tried to do filing, but papers got lost. She was fun to be with, though. The two women became good friends, and Zora continued to work for Ms. Hurst—but as her driver and companion.

Unfortunately, when the two women went out

Zora said, "I love myself when I am laughing. . . ." (State Archives of Florida, Florida Memory, http://floridamemory.com/items/show/33048)

together, the difference in their skin color caused problems. Since some restaurants were "Whites Only" or "Colored Only," these two women were not supposed to sit together.

At one restaurant, afraid that the headwaiter would refuse to seat them, Ms. Hurst calmly explained that Zora was an African princess and she didn't see any reason that the two women shouldn't be seated at the same table. Not only did the headwaiter allow them in, but he gave them one of the best tables in the restaurant. They had their fun, but Zora was sad to think that she was not welcome simply because of the color of her skin.

Chapter 6

College at Last

At the banquet, Zora met another well-known writer, Annie Nathan Meyer. She was one of the founders of Barnard College, a college for women in New York City. When they met, Ms. Meyer realized there was more to Zora than just a lovely personality. She realized she was a very intelligent woman.

Thanks to Ms. Meyer, Zora would finally be able to finish her college education with a scholarship to Barnard. In the fall of 1925, Zora entered Barnard College at the age of 34 (although she probably said she was younger!). When she graduated in 1928, she was only the second black student to graduate from that excellent school.

Zora chose a lot of English and history courses

Zora's graduation photo from Barnard College (Courtesy of Barnard College Archives)

until her adviser suggested that she try a course in anthropology. Anthropology is the study of people and the way they live. This course changed Zora's life.

Her teacher was Dr. Franz Boas, one of the leading anthropologists in the United States. Boas immediately realized that he had the perfect student in Zora Neale Hurston. She was African-American. She was a writer. With some training in anthropology, she would be perfectly suited for writing down the ways of African-Americans living in the South.

The job of an anthropologist is to understand and preserve information about how groups of people live. And with America's cities growing so quickly in those days, small groups of African-Americans living throughout the

South would soon be gone. Gone were the dirt roads of Zora's childhood in Eatonville. Cities and paved roads were changing the way blacks had lived for years.

Dr. Boas did not study people to see if one group was superior or inferior to others. He wanted facts. Each group is special and fascinating in its own way.

Franz Boas believed that Zora could make a huge contribution to American history by visiting African-American communities in Southern states and bringing back information about how they lived, what stories they told about their own lives, and even songs they sang. All of these things were called the "folklore" of the people. Zora would be writing down some stories like the ones she had heard on the porch of Joe Clarke's store. And those stories, Zora remembered, were such fun to listen to.

Other people had tried to gather African-American folklore in the South, but it had not yet been done by someone of the same race. Zora became the first college-trained African-American anthropologist at that time. She was unique. As a scientist as well as a writer, she had found a way to use all of her talents.

Before graduation, Dr. Boas obtained a fellowship for Zora in the amount of $1,400 to pay for a trip to the South. What she had learned in the classroom would now be put into practice.

The Association for the Study of Negro Life and History and the American Folklore Society paid the bills, and Dr. Boas guided her work. Zora was to travel from Florida to Louisiana, and she was anxious to get started.

Taking a train to Jacksonville, Florida, she stopped for a short time to buy a car, which she named "Sassy Susie." On this trip, she went even farther than America's Southern states. She also made a quick boat trip to Nassau in the Bahama Islands.

Zora returned to New York very disappointed, however. She had been well trained at Barnard. She understood her people. But as she drove from one group to another, she didn't get much cooperation. She asked to hear their songs and stories, and they told her some, and she wrote them down. But something was missing. She wasn't feeling the spirit of the people. She thought she had failed.

It was not failure, however. She was just learning how to do something that no one like her had done before.

Chapter 7

Collecting Folklore

After graduation, Zora was anxious to go back to see if she could do a better job. She knew that there was plenty of information out there. She said it was "disappearing without the world ever realizing that it ever had been." But she had no money for another trip.

One of her friends, the poet Langston Hughes, mentioned that he was being helped by Mrs. Charlotte Mason, a woman who was willing to help African-American artists and writers. Zora met with Ms. Mason and gladly signed a contract that would give Zora $200 a month for expenses while collecting folklore. Zora would be able to make another trip South!

There would be problems in the future with that

Zora, Rochelle French, and Gabriel Brown (playing guitar) in Eatonville, Florida, 1935 (State Archives of Florida, Florida Memory, http:// floridamemory.com/items/show/107444)

contract, however. Yes, Ms. Mason's money would pay her bills, but Zora would not have the rights to the folklore she collected. Her research became Ms. Mason's property. Zora would be limited by Ms. Mason's approval as to how to use all of the wonderful stories she collected, so it would not be until years later that any of her books would be published.

Ms. Mason also wanted to know how every dollar was spent. Toothpaste and shampoo and other necessary items all had to be written down. One month, Zora waited until the last minute to buy a new pair of shoes. Her toes were bursting through the old ones, and she couldn't put that expense off any longer.

But at least Zora could travel. As soon as she could, she took a train headed south from New York City. She stayed for 16 months, and this trip went much better.

She realized now that "(t)he glamo(u)r of Barnard College" was still upon her during her first trip. She had driven a shiny car into poor communities and asked to hear the songs and stories of the people. They had looked at her in her nice clothes and at her car. They had known immediately that, although she was African-American, she did not belong there.

Yes, she was a Barnard College graduate. Yes, she was a famous author. But she now realized that she had to blend in with the people living in the poor Southern communities. She needed to become one of them again. She said later: "I had to go back, dress as they did, talk as they did, live their life."

This worked. She explained the car as a present from a friend. She dressed in plainer clothes. She accepted their ways, and they accepted her. She didn't just ask questions. She would observe and remember. Later, alone, she would write everything down on paper. She wrote in great detail, even down to the dialect, or the way the people pronounced their words.

When invited, she stayed at someone's home overnight. Of course, that did not always make for a good night's sleep. The beds were sometimes very uncomfortable, and some of them were loaded with bedbugs!

She enjoyed the work, but it was not easy. She looked for out-of-the-way places where African-Americans still lived in small groups, away from the cities. She found them living in shacks on the edge of a large citrus grove, waiting to harvest the oranges. She found them in lumber camps in the deep woods. She was a single woman, and sometimes her life was in danger. Once a woman thought her boyfriend was paying too much attention to Zora, and Zora had to leave very quickly!

Driving from state to state, Zora sometimes had to stay at a hotel overnight. That too was a challenge. She had to find one for "colored people." No matter what kind of important research she was doing or how many years she had spent in a university, she was still African-American and not welcome in "Whites Only" hotels. She found hotels that accepted people of her race, or she slept in her car.

She had so many fascinating experiences, and she either wrote them down or they stayed in her memory.

One time, while studying the blacks living in the Bahama Islands, a hurricane hit with tremendous force. The experience was frightening. As soon as she could, she wrote in her notes the sights, the sounds, and the fear.

Ms. Mason might get the folklore she had collected, but the memory of the whistling wind through the bending palm trees and the ocean water blowing through the air around her would stay with Zora. When she later wrote her book *Their Eyes Were Watching God*, she could describe that experience so clearly that her readers knew she had been through a real storm herself.

This time, and on future trips, Zora's collecting of folklore went very well.

Chapter 8

Writing Stories

Zora loved her work. She once said, "I want to collect like a new broom."

In 1931 some of Zora's folklore stories were published in the *Journal of American Folklore*. With Ms. Mason's approval, Zora also worked with Langston Hughes on a play based on her folklore called *Mule Bone*.

But it was the time of the Great Depression, and many people were out of work. Zora too went through a hard time. Her help from Ms. Mason was mostly done, but she still needed to write stories. The challenge was always to pay her bills while still using her talent.

Mary McLeod Bethune had started a school for girls in Daytona Beach, Florida, and offered Zora the job of setting up a school of dramatic arts there. But Zora was best at writing, not setting up schools, so she soon went back to what she really loved.

A professor at Rollins College in Winter Park, Florida, wanting to interest his students in American folk life, read one of Zora's stories, "The Gilded Six-Bits." He was so impressed with her writing that he sent it to *Story* magazine. The story was published in the August 1933 issue. Zora was paid $20 for it, and it created another opportunity for her. Four national publishers read the story, liked it, and asked if she had started a novel, a story long enough to be made into a book. Although she had not yet put the words on paper, Zora did have the idea for a novel. She told publisher Bertram Lippincott of J.B. Lippincott Company that yes, she did.

She went to work immediately, ignoring any interruptions. Later, she would explain her life at this time by saying, "There is no agony like bearing an untold story inside you." She rented a small house in Sanford, Florida, for $1.50 a week and concentrated completely on her writing. She even ignored the landlady knocking on her door looking for rent. Friends stopped by to make sure that at least she was eating.

Her novel just flowed from inside of her. The main characters were John and Lucy, the names of her parents, and it was a story based on their marriage. It was titled *Jonah's Gourd Vine* and was written by hand in pencil.

When it was finished, she had no money at all. She asked a typist to type it for her and asked a friend to lend her $1.83 for postage to send it to Lippincott's Philadelphia office. The manuscript was sent on October 3, 1933. Then she waited.

Unfortunately, the landlady was also waiting. Two weeks later, on October 16, at 8 in the morning, Zora answered a knock on her door. It was the landlady, and she wanted her rent money immediately. Zora had just gotten a job and would have been able to pay her later that afternoon, but the landlady wanted her $18 in back rent right then. Zora had to move out of the house before going to work for the day.

Just hours later, a telegram reached Zora from Bertram Lippincott. He would not only publish *Jonah's Gourd Vine,* but he offered to give her $200 as an advance from book sales. Although she was homeless, Zora could not have been happier. She said later: "I never expect to have a greater thrill than that wire gave me."

Jonah's Gourd Vine was published in May 1934, and *The New York Times* newspaper called the book "the most vital and original novel about the American Negro that has yet been written by a member of the Negro race."

That was a high compliment for a first novel.

The flow of books had started. Zora's next book, *Mules and Men,* a collection of the folklore she had collected, was published in late 1935. Traveling to the Caribbean island of Haiti, she wrote a love story that she said was "dammed up" within her. She had to immediately sit and write it, and the entire book was finished in just seven weeks! That book was *Their Eyes Were Watching God,* and it was published in 1937. Bertram Lippincott called Zora "a natural writer," and this story has been called a "masterpiece."

Tell My Horse, another book of folklore, followed in October 1938, and her next novel was *Moses, Man of the Mountain,* which she struggled with for four years. This book was interesting but not about the subject she knew so well.

Writing was not always easy for Zora. There was still much segregation in America, and some African-Americans thought she should be writing about the problems of the day. But Zora wanted to write stories that anyone would understand, that would be read and enjoyed by all races. To those who criticized her work, she said, "What I wanted to tell was a story about a man, and from what I read and heard, Negroes were supposed to write about the Race Problem. I was and am thoroughly

*Postcard photo of Zora (State Archives of Florida, Florida Memory, http://
floridamemory.com/items/show/17244, photographed by Carl Van Vechten)*

sick of the subject. My interest lies in what makes a man
. . . do such-and-so, regardless of his color."

By 1941, many people had read Zora's books, and
Bertram Lippincott asked Zora to write her autobiography.
She hesitated, because she wanted to write stories, not
facts about her own life. She finally agreed, and when
Dust Tracks on a Road was published in November 1942,
her many readers learned about the interesting life of
this 51-year-old African-American woman writer from a
small town in Florida called Eatonville.

Chapter 9

The Famous Author

Zora was a successful author. She had received an honorary Doctor of Letters degree from Morgan State College and a Distinguished Alumni Award from Howard University. Later, she would accept an award for "education and human relations" at Bethune-Cookman College.

Her autobiography won the 1943 Anisfield-Wolf Award in Race Relations and $1,000 from the magazine *Saturday Review of Literature*. The magazine said it helped people of other races to understand more clearly the African-American culture. *Saturday Review of Literature* also featured Zora on the cover of its February 20, 1943, issue.

The award finally allowed her to buy a home—on

water. She bought a 20-year-old houseboat called the *Wanago,* fixed it up, and soon was chugging up and down the waters near Daytona Beach in Florida. It was a lovely change from all of the moving around she had done previously. She was happy.

She became friends with another writer at that time, Marjorie Kinnan Rawlings, who lived at Cross Creek in north central Florida. Marjorie became so interested in the people who had lived for years at Cross Creek that she started writing about them. Those people were called Crackers. Her book *The Yearling,* about a boy in the Florida woods and his pet deer, won a Pulitzer Prize.

One day Marjorie invited Zora to come for a visit at her husband's hotel in St. Augustine. Zora, realizing that the hotel was for white guests only, took a back stairway instead of the guest elevator up to Marjorie's apartment on the top floor. Once she was there, the two women thoroughly enjoyed their visit. Although they were of different races, they had much in common.

Zora still sent articles to magazines and, when invited, gave talks to groups. Speaking at a meeting in Belle Glade, Florida, she met Sara Lee Creech. Sara mentioned a concern she had. Although there were dolls that looked like white children, there were no dolls that looked like young African-American girls. Ms. Creech wanted to find a company that would manufacture the dolls.

Zora asked some of her famous friends to convince a doll manufacturer of the need for these special dolls. Zora also suggested that the new doll's name be Sara Lee. In 1951 Sears, Roebuck and Company sold the

The Sara Lee doll (Courtesy of The Strong®, Rochester, New York)

baby dolls, and young African-American girls then had a doll—the Sara Lee Doll—that looked like them.

Zora's next novel, *Seraph on the Suwanee,* was published in October 1948 by a new publisher, Scribner's. Although *Seraph* received some good reviews, Zora had the worst time of her life just before the book was published.

On September 13, 1948, the New York City police arrested Zora. A woman had accused Zora of improper behavior with her son. Zora was innocent. She wasn't even in New York when the boy said that she did this. But when the case went to court, newspapers took up the story. What should have been a happy time, with her new book being published, turned into something terrible for her.

Much of the money from her book sales went to the lawyers who defended her in court. Again, Zora had no money to live on. Magazine articles paid some of her bills, but she wrote to a friend saying she was ". . . inching along like a stepped-on worm from day to day. Borrowing a little here and there."

When she received $1,000 for an article she wrote for the *Saturday Evening Post,* she moved into a small, one-room house with Spot, a little brown and white terrier dog she had adopted. When the owner of the house decided to sell it to someone else, Zora made her final move, to Fort Pierce, Florida. There she had been offered work as a part-time writer for the local newspaper, *The Fort Pierce Chronicle.*

Her health was not good. Dr. C.C. Benton, a black physician in Fort Pierce, was not only her doctor but a very good friend. He had grown up near Eatonville and had known Zora's father, John Hurston. Dr. Benton allowed Zora to live rent-free in a home he owned, and he invited her to his house for dinner each Sunday.

Zora enjoyed telling stories to the neighborhood

Zora (middle) with friends, Fort Pierce, Florida, 1959 (Zora Neale Hurston Papers, Department of Special and Area Studies Collections, George A. Smathers Libraries, University of Florida)

children and always told them to be proud of their race. In her flower garden, she planted Cape Jasmine bushes. They were just as lovely—and smelled just as sweet—as the ones grown in her parents' yard in Eatonville years before.

After having a stroke in early 1959, her heart was weak and she could no longer stay at home. She was admitted to the segregated St. Lucie County Welfare Home, where she died on January 28, 1960. She was 69 years old.

Cape Jasmine bloom (Sandra Sammons)

Marjorie Silver, one of her friends, wrote an article about Zora for the *Miami Herald*, and newspapers around the country picked up the news of Zora's death. Friends sent money to pay for a funeral. On Sunday, February 7, 1960, at 3 in the afternoon, there were so many flower arrangements and so many people at the funeral service that chairs had to be set up on the sidewalk outside the church.

In honoring this great writer's life during the service, the Reverend Wayman A. Jennings said, "They said she couldn't become a writer recognized by the world. But she did it. The Miami paper said she died poor. But she died rich. She did something."

Truly, this was a woman who did "jump at de sun."

Afterword

Zora Neale Hurston died poor in money, but she definitely "did something." For 30 years she wrote stories that she thought were important. That little town of Eatonville gave her confidence, and throughout her life she was proud to be an African-American. Just 70 years after black people were bound in slavery and were not allowed to be educated, Zora graduated from Barnard College in New York City.

When she died, she was buried in an unmarked

grave. Zora could easily have been forgotten. But 13 years later, Alice Walker, an African-American writer who won the Pulitzer Prize for her novel *The Color Purple*, learned about Zora in a class she was taking.

Alice Walker signing books at the Zora Neale Hurston Festival, Eatonville, Florida, 1990 (State Archives of Florida, Florida Memory, http://floridamemory.com/items/ show/106463, collection of Nancy Nusz)

She was amazed at the quality of her writing and was determined to find Zora's grave.

In August 1973, Ms. Walker searched for the gravesite and found only weeds. So she erected a gravestone in the cemetery in Zora's memory. The writing on the gray stone says:

ZORA NEALE HURSTON
"A GENIUS OF THE SOUTH"
1901–1960
NOVELIST, FOLKLORIST
ANTHROPOLOGIST

Today, Zora's novel *Their Eyes Were Watching God* is considered a masterpiece of literature. Her books have been translated into Spanish, French, Italian, German, Japanese, and other languages. In 2005 Oprah Winfrey's film version of the book starred Halle Berry and Ruby Dee. Spike Lee also used some of Zora's words from *Their Eyes Were Watching God* at the beginning of his 1986 film, *She's Gotta Have It*.

Her hometown of Eatonville has a Zora Neale Hurston Museum and a Zora Neale Hurston Library. In Fort Pierce, her home is now a National Historic Landmark, and there is a Zora Neale Hurston Dust Tracks Heritage Trail.

Tents at the Zora Neale Hurston Festival, Eatonville, Florida, 1990
(State Archives of Florida, Florida Memory, http://floridamemory.com/items/
show/106470, collection of Jill Linzee)

Zora's life has been an inspiration not just to many African-American women but to women of other races as well. Her stories are about subjects we all understand. Fannie Hurst summed up her friend's life well when she said that Zora was "a gift to both her race and the human race."

Zora Neale Hurston, talented African-American author, will not be forgotten.

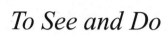

To See and Do

New York City
Schomburg Center for Research in Black Culture
The New York Public Library
515 Malcolm X Blvd
New York, NY 10037-1801
212-491-2200
www.nypl.org/locations/schomburg

Located in Harlem, this is a research unit of the New York Public Library. It offers free programs and exhibitions.

Fort Pierce, Florida
The Garden of Heavenly Rest Cemetery
At the end of 17th Street (heading north)
Fort Pierce, FL 34950

Zora Neale Hurston Library
3008 Avenue D

Fort Pierce, FL 34947
772-462-2154

Eatonville, Florida
Robert Hungerford Elementary School
230 S. College Avenue
Eatonville, FL 32751

The Macedonia Missionary Baptist Church
412 East Kennedy Blvd.
Eatonville, FL 32751
407-647-0010
www.mdonia.org

The Zora Neale Hurston Museum
227 East Kennedy Blvd.
Eatonville, FL 32751
407-647-3307
www.zoranealehurstonmuseum.com

Zora! Festival of the Arts and Humanities
Annually; last week in January
407-647-3307
www.zorafestival.org

Glossary

astonish – to surprise

Cape Jasmine flowers – white, sweet-smelling flowers; also called gardenias

dialect – a variety of a language that is spoken by a particular group or spoken in a certain part of a country

discrimination – the unfair treatment of a certain group of people; prejudice

dramatic arts – writing theater plays; the art of acting

fellowship – a grant of money, usually to do studies or research

folklore – literature transmitted verbally

gourd – a plant with a hard shell like a pumpkin or squash

Great Depression – a time during the 1930s when many people were out of work

incorporated – made legal, such as a city

migration – movement from one place to another

glamor – charm

literary – having to do with books or literature

mythology – a collection of stories about the gods and legendary heroes of a particular people

operetta – a play with some talk and some singing

plantation – a large farm

publish – to print and distribute someone's book

racism – a belief that one's own race is superior

renaissance – renewal, or a time of rebirth of interest in art and learning in a society

scholarship – money given to students so they may take classes at a college or university

segregation – the policy of keeping people of different races separate, as in schools, housing, industry

seraph – angel

urban – having to do with cities

wire – telegram

Selected Bibliography

Candaele, Kerry. *Bound for Glory: From the Great Migration to the Harlem Renaissance, 1910–1930.* New York: Chelsea House Publishers, 1996.

Hurston, Lucy. *Speak, So You Can Speak Again: The Life of Zora Neale Hurston.* New York: Doubleday, 2004.

Witcover, Paul. *Zora Neale Hurston: Author.* New York: Chelsea House Publishers, 1991.

References

Note: "Ibid." is short for the Latin word *ibidem,* which means "in the same place." If you see "ibid.," that means that a quote came from the same book as the quote before it did.

Foreword

"Sometimes, I feel discriminated against . . .": Valerie Boyd, *Wrapped in Rainbows: The Life of Zora Neale Hurston* (New York: Scribner, 2003), 145.

"one of the greatest writers of the twentieth century": Lucy Anne Hurston, *Speak, So You Can Speak Again* (New York: Doubleday, 2004), 6.

Chapter 1

"I am so put together . . .": Deborah G. Plant, ed., *"The Inside Light": New Critical Essays on Zora Neale Hurston* (Westport, CT: Praeger, 2010), 206.

Chapter 2

"squinch": Zora Neale Hurston, *Dust Tracks on a Road: An Autobiography* (New York: Harper Perennial Modern Classics, reprint, 2010), 13.

"It [does] not do for Negroes . . .": Ibid., 13.

"jump at de sun": Ibid., 13.

"We might not land . . .": Ibid., 13.

"travel dust": Ibid., 23.

"all blue and pink . . .": Zora Neale Hurston, *Dust Tracks on a Road: An Autobiography*, 53.

"It blowed a crooked road . . .": Janelle Yates. *Zora Neale Hurston: A Storyteller's Life* (Staten Island, NY: Ward Hill Press, 1993), 10.

"True, I played, fought . . .": Zora Neale Hurston, *Dust Tracks on a Road: An Autobiography*, 43.

"My soul was with the gods . . .": Ibid., 41.

Chapter 3

"Mama died at sundown . . .": Zora Neale Hurston, *Dust Tracks on a Road: An Autobiography*, 67.

Jacksonville made me know . . .": Ibid., 70.

"an unnecessary evil": Ibid., 79.

"I was doing none . . .": Ibid., 97.

"I had a way of life . . .": Ibid., 100.

Chapter 4

"I acted as if . . .": Zora Neale Hurston, *Dust Tracks on a Road: An Autobiography,* 124.

"Every new thing . . .": Ibid., 129.

"I felt the ladder . . .": Ibid., 131.

"little brown figure . . .": Zora Neale Hurston, "Drenched in Light." *Opportunity,* December 1924.

Chapter 5

"When Zora was there . . .": Steven Watson, *The Harlem Renaissance: Hub of African-American Culture, 1920–1930* (New York: Pantheon, 1996), 71.

"I am just running wild . . .": Ibid., 71.

"I love myself . . .": Paul Witcover, *Zora Neale Hurston: Author* (New York: Chelsea House Publishers, 1991), 73.

Chapter 7

"disappearing without . . .": Robert E. Hemenway, *Zora Neale Hurston: A Literary Biography* (Champaign: University of Illinois Press, 1977), 108.

"(t)he glamo(u)r . . .": Zora Neale Hurston, *Dust Tracks on a Road: An Autobiography,* 143.

"I had to go back . . .": Mary E. Lyons, *Sorrow's Kitchen: The Life and Folklore of Zora Neale Hurston* (New York: Atheneum Books for Young Readers, 1993), 64.

Chapter 8

"I want to collect . . .": Valerie Boyd, *Wrapped in Rainbows: The Life of Zora Neale Hurston,* 162.

"There is no agony . . .": Zora Neale Hurston, *Dust Tracks on a Road: An Autobiography,* 176.

"I never expect . . .": Ibid., 175.

"the most vital . . .": Review by Margaret Wallace, *The New York Times,* May 6, 1934.

"dammed up": Zora Neale Hurston, *Dust Tracks on a Road: An Autobiography,* 175.

"a natural writer": Valerie Boyd, *Wrapped in Rainbows: The Life of Zora Neale Hurston,* 297.

"masterpiece": Paul Witcover, *Zora Neale Hurston: Author,* 99.

"What I wanted to tell . . .": Zora Neale Hurston, *Dust Tracks on a Road: An Autobiography,* 171.

Chapter 9

"inching along . . .": Mary E. Lyons, *Sorrow's Kitchen: The Life and Folklore of Zora Neale Hurston,* 110.

"They said she couldn't . . .": Valerie Boyd, *Wrapped in Rainbows: The Life of Zora Neale Hurston,* 433.

Afterword

"a gift to both . . .": Virginia Lynn Moylan, *Zora Neale Hurston's Final Decade* (Gainesville: University Press of Florida, 2011), 161.

Acknowledgments

It's hard to believe that I actually started my manuscript on Zora more than 20 years ago. I had sent that copy to Robert Hemenway, who wrote a complete biography of this wonderful woman, and he encouraged me to get my book published. It didn't happen then, but the time has come. I want to give my first thanks to all of the fine people at Pineapple Press for encouraging me to finally finish it and put it into print.

I also want to thank the following people for reading over my work: Benjamin DiBiase of the Florida Historical Society; Maye St. Julien, chairperson of the Historic Preservation Board of the Town of Eatonville; friends Randall and Barbara Shew and Phyllis Lewis; Ashley Birchfield, seventh-grade student at the Thomas Jefferson Classical Academy, Henrietta, North Carolina; and my husband, Bob Sammons. Their expertise is appreciated. Any errors that crept in I accept as my own.

Index

About the Author

Sandra Wallus Sammons and her husband live in a house surrounded by a large garden, like Zora's, full of vegetables and flowers.

Here are some other books from Pineapple Press that might interest you. For a complete catalog, write to Pineapple Press, P.O. Box 3889, Sarasota, Florida 34230-3889, or call (800) 746-3275. Or visit our website at www.pineapplepress.com.

Ponce de Leon and the Discovery of Florida by Sandra Wallus Sammons. In 1513 Juan Ponce de Leon sailed into the unknown to discover new lands. He stopped at one place that seemed to be an island but that was really part of a whole new continent. He named it "La Florida." Ages 9–12.

Marjory Stoneman Douglas and the Florida Everglades by Sandra Wallus Sammons. Called the "grandmother of the Everglades," Marjory Stoneman Douglas was a tireless crusader for the preservation of the famed River of Grass. Read about her childhood up North and her long and inspiring life in Florida. Ages 9–12.

Marjorie Kinnan Rawlings and the Florida Crackers by Sandra Wallus Sammons. Marjorie Kinnan Rawlings grew up hoping to become an author. When she moved to Florida, she met the so-called Crackers and wrote stories about them. Her novel *The Yearling* won the Pulitzer Prize for fiction. Ages 9–12.

The Two Henrys by Sandra Wallus Sammons. Henry Flagler and Henry Plant changed the landscape of Florida in the late 1800s and early 1900s. This dual biography is the story of railroads and the men who built them. Flagler opened up Florida's east coast with his railroads and hotels, and Plant did the same on the west coast. Age 12 and up.

Henry Flagler, Builder of Florida by Sandra Wallus Sammons. An exciting biography about the man who changed Florida's east coast. Already a millionaire when he first visited Florida in 1878, Henry Flagler later returned and built railroads and hotels to open up the coast to visitors. By 1912 he had built a railroad all the way to Key West. Ages 9–12.

Those Amazing Animals series. Each book in this series includes 20 questions and answers about an animal, 20 photos, and 20 funny illustrations. Learn about alligators, bears, flamingos, turtles, vultures, and many more. Ages 5–9.

Olivia Brophie and the Pearl of Tagelus by Chris Tozier. Fantasy fiction. Olivia Brophie's dad has sent her to live with her eccentric aunt and uncle in the Florida scrub. Life is boring until bears follow her to school and tree frogs start writing cryptic messages on her bedroom window. Olivia slips down a tortoise burrow into the vast Floridan aquifer, where ancient animals thrive in a mysterious world. Age 8 and up.

Olivia Brophie and the Sky Island by Chris Tozier. Second book in the Olivia Brophie series. Olivia's life is in turmoil ever since she accidentally froze all of the earth's water and her aunt and uncle were kidnapped by the Wardenclyffe thugs. With the help of a black bear named Hoolie, she must travel across America to undo the damage she caused. Meanwhile, Doug and Gnat are drawn deeper into the world of Junonia, the mysterious city beneath the Floridan aquifer. Age 8 and up.

Iguana Invasion! Exotic Pets Gone Wild in Florida by Virginia Aronson and Allyn Szejko. Green iguanas, Burmese pythons, Nile monitor lizards, rhesus monkeys, and many more non-native animals are rapidly increasing in population in subtropical Florida. This full-color book provides scientific information, exciting wildlife stories, and photos for the most common exotic animals on the loose, most of them offspring of abandoned pets. Age 12 and up.

The Gopher Tortoise by Ray and Patricia Ashton. Explains the critical role this tortoise and its burrow play in the upland ecosystem of Florida and the Southeast. Learn how scientists study this animal and try to protect it. Age 10 and up.

My Florida Facts by Russell and Annie Johnson. Learn facts about Florida, from the state capital to the number of counties, from what states border Florida to how to make a Key lime pie. A kid-friendly book that makes learning fun by singing along with the "My Florida Facts" song, included on a CD. Ages 8–12.

The Crafts of Florida's First People by Robin Brown. Learn how the earliest Indians got their food, made clothing, and cooked meals by doing these things the way they did, using materials you can find in Florida today. Includes illustrated instructions on how to make pottery, weave cloth, build traps, start a fire without matches, and more. Age 10 and up.

America's REAL First Thanksgiving by Robyn Gioia. When most Americans think of the first Thanksgiving, they think of the Pilgrims and the Indians in New England in 1621. But on September 8, 1565, the Spanish and the native Timucua celebrated with a feast of Thanksgiving in St. Augustine. Teacher's activity guide also available. Ages 9–14.